Passive Income:
Guide to Create Multiple Income Streams

Without Having to Work for it

Success Publishing

Text Copyright © [Success Publishing]

All rights reserved. No part of this guide may be reproduced in any form without permission in writing from the publisher except in the case of brief quotations embodied in critical articles or reviews.

Legal & Disclaimer

The information contained in this book and its contents is not designed to replace or take the place of any form of medical or professional advice; and is not meant to replace the need for independent medical, financial, legal or other professional advice or services, as may be required. The content and information in this book have been provided for educational and entertainment purposes only.

The content and information contained in this book have been compiled from sources deemed reliable, and it is accurate to the best of the Author's knowledge, information, and belief. However, the Author cannot guarantee its accuracy and validity and cannot be held liable for any errors and/or omissions. Further, changes are periodically made to this book as and when needed. Where appropriate and/or necessary, you must consult a professional (including but not limited to your doctor, attorney, financial advisor or such other professional advisor) before using any of the suggested remedies, techniques, or information in this book.

Upon using the contents and information contained in this book, you agree to hold harmless the Author from and against any damages, costs, and expenses, including any legal fees potentially resulting from the application of any of the information provided by this book. This disclaimer applies to any loss, damages or injury caused by the use and application, whether directly or indirectly, of any advice or information presented, whether for breach of contract, tort, negligence, personal injury, criminal intent, or under any other cause of action.

You agree to accept all risks of using the information presented inside this book.

You agree that by continuing to read this book, where appropriate and/or necessary, you shall consult a professional (including but not limited to your doctor, attorney, or financial advisor or such other advisor as needed) before using any of the suggested remedies, techniques, or information in this book.

Table of Contents

Introduction 5

Chapter 1 – Difference Between Passive Income and Active Income 6

Chapter 2 – What is Passive Income and its Benefits 8

These are just few of all the benefits that you can receive through passive income. Learn what the phases of passive income are to get started living to your freedom while earning money without a need to work for it. 9

Chapter 3 – How Can a Passive Income be Generated? 10

Chapter 4 - Phases Passive Income 13

Chapter 5 – Sources of Passive Income 15

    Passive Income Requiring Upfront Time Investment 15

    Passive Income Requiring Upfront Monetary Investment 16

    Semi-Passive Small Business 17

    Easy Passive Income Ideas 18

    Online Passive Income Sources 18

Chapter 6 –How to Spot A Passive Income Opportunity 20

Chapter 7 –Building Passive Income As an Established Marketer 22

Conclusion 24

Also, Check Out This Other Book Published by Success Publishing 25

Free Preview Bonus 26

CHAPTER 1: Reasons for Getting Into an Online 27

Business 27

    Goodbye to Traffic and Early Morning Rush 27

    No Need Putting Up with a Toxic Boss 27

Working at your own Pace and Time 27

Unlimited Income Potential 28

Minimal Expenses for an Office 28

Bigger Chance to Achieve more for Less Work 28

Common Problems you will Encounter at the Start of your Online Business 29

    Tempting Opportunities and Resources 29

    Neglecting New Opportunities 29

    Doing Everything by Yourself 29

    Having Too Many Choices 29

    The Internet is Bigger than What You Think 30

    No Support from Family and Friend 30

Introduction

In the present economic climate, it has been more important to not just work hard but also have your money work harder for you. Almost everyone is putting in many hours at their place of employment. Nevertheless, in the past several years, the job market fails to provide the stability and security that people are looking for. Jobs that are usually relied on by families are gone with lots of pundits proclaiming them being defunct.

Aside from that, lots of people question the effectiveness of stock market to grow their retirement funds when it comes to recent subsequent and crash volatility. Because most of the trusted institutions like stock market and job market have collapsed, people are looking for alternative ways to entrust their hard-earned money into, to help in growing their wealth. These days, more and more people realize the significance of finding sources of passive income to help in supplementing or replacing the earned income from their jobs.

The internet has become a wealth of information to millions of people and it has been a major source of income for them, creating a new industry that generates many jobs and becoming an opportunity for most people to receive profits directly on the web. These people have even left their day jobs to put their focus on working full time online when they realized that they earn more as compared to what they used to get.

In addition, they discovered the benefits of making money online ultimately overweight all the involved risks. Thousands of internet users usually wonder if it is possible to generate passive income on the web. Most particularly those who do not have experience or skills commonly become thundered listening to the many success stories. Nonetheless, this book is designed to help those who seek to build passive income without having to work for it.

Making passive income has not been a fantasy anymore. People make millions every month from all over the world. There is no need to spend a great deal of money to work into making money online. What you need to do is consider several ideas to get money online without a need to spend a dime or the need to work for it. Thousands of online marketers who did not have any technical knowledge now earn their breads on the web. They did not know anything with regards to passive income generation, but they found a guide that helps them succeed.

Chapter 1 – Difference Between Passive Income and Active Income

In making money online, there are 2 types: the active income and the passive income. You may have already known that there is a difference between the two and you may have also known that it is likely that you do not really grasp the implications of these differences. There is nothing wrong with either of them but if you are into maximizing your returns, you would want to ensure that you have a solid feel for what is the difference between the two.

Active income is one for which services are performed, including tips, commissions, wages, salaries, and income from businesses with material participation. On the other hand, passive income is an earning derived by people from a limited partnership, rental property, or other enterprise wherein he/she is not involved actively. Passive income does not include earnings from active business participation, whereas the active income involves doing something to be able to receive an income, including some sort of effort or work. You are not hands-off. You will need to exert some type of time and energy into earning that income. Passive income means earning income on a regular basis without any necessary efforts to keep it coming.

Your Goals versus your Source of Income

You may be wondering why it matters on which one you are earning if it is all income. This is because accomplishing your goals will vary on having an understanding about these terms very clearly. You need to know that the most common reason why investors are getting into real estate investing is the financial freedom. People who seek for financial freedom define goal as having the capability to use real estate as a vehicle for breaking loose of their current career and not have to work for their income.

Financial freedom means you do not need to do any works to be able to receive income, so as soon as you are financially free, you do not need to worry about money any longer. Perhaps you are planning to do lots of traveling, it is recommended to take random college courses and learn new things for fun, not because you need to. You may also take up new hobbies, or spend great amount of time playing in the woods and snowboarding. Alternatively, maybe you are planning to wake up early and hang out with your kids at home all day. These situations are called lifestyle design. You can design your life exactly how you want it to be. If you are planning to stay at your present job, you are not into lifestyle design. Through financial freedom, you will be able to do anything you want.

Investment Methods: Active vs. Passive

In real estate investing, there are broad categories that someone can get involved with. Between these categories, it splits into 50/50 on which ones are producing active income and which ones are producing passive income. The investments on active income include wholesaling and flipping. You will need to do work to be able to see money from them. There is a need to be hands-on. On the other hand, the investments on passive income include paper/notes and rental properties. If done in the right way, both can provide earnings for you no matter if you are hands off or on.

The real difference between the two

Active income investing is typically a job. Lots of people do not see it like that but it really is. House flipping is a job. Landlording a rental property is a job. And, wholesaling is a job. It is great significant to have an understanding because it is difference on how you spend your time. Huge investors are making money in their sleep without a need put in any efforts because they are investing in a passive income investment. If you would out in lots of efforts while making bank, you are working.

You make so much income because you rock out a job. Also, big investors are putting in so much effort but their efforts are not on what makes the income for them, but rather about on finding the next thing that provides more income to them. If you like the job of flipping, wholesaling, or landlording, or anything that you do actively to be able to earn income, you will have to rock on with it. More particularly if you are planning to use that job to purchase passive investments, which has been the way one become successful, it is advisable to find ways into financial freedom.

In line with that, you may work on any job or you can decide to build a business to earn income to be used for investing in passive income. It does not need to be landlording, flipping, or wholesaling. You may learn so much about investments working these jobs, but it can be a job that you want completely outside of real estate if you want it to be. Real estate has been a fantastic way of earning fat cash, and therefore lots of people are sticking with it. Furthermore, if you are doing that, you are still great, if you realize that you are working a job.

These come down to your goals. There is no wrong thing about wholesaling, landlording, or flipping, if you understand the fact, and that you are okay with that fact that you are working for your money. In line with this, it is highly recommended to stick with investing to passive income. However, you should have a business startup if you want to fund your investments. You can do anything you want, but be clear on what you do, between working for your money or investing your money.

Chapter 2 – What is Passive Income and its Benefits

Passive income is considered money that is generated by any business or trade. It is also considered an income-producing activity that people do not participate in directly. For instance, the paid royalties to an author from their published book would be considered passive income. Another example of passive income is when you write a song and received royalties for your efforts. However, the likelihood of succeeding as a songwriter or author has not been a viable choice for most people. Also, there are many online systems that are geared into generating ongoing streams of income. Things ranging from blogging to affiliate marketing was touted as the definite way for supplementing their income or escaping their day job. In other cases, passive income may also be derived from owning assets like real estate business.

Earning passive income puts you on the advantage over the other people who have been making online through working for other people. If you want to own a wealthy and healthy lifestyle, there is no need for you to make money depending only on your 9-5 jobs. Rather, you would want to set up a passive income system. Passive income provides many advantages that cannot be provided by common 9-5 jobs. Also, these benefits do not just enable you to have more freedom, but also become richer. However, giving you a chance to retire being wealthy.

Unlimited Income

Among the greatest issues that you will find with a job is that there will always be a ceiling. Regardless of how hard you work, and about how many raises you receive, there will always be limit given to a job. Through online businesses like internet marketing and other MLM options, there will be no limit. if you want to work 10 hours per day on this and want to pull seven figure yearly earnings, no one will stop you. You are removing the limits when you have a passive solution to your income. You will be able to create as much wealth as you want and you may do so through proven techniques that many others work on right now. You will not be limited to the notion of limits, or any ceiling of wages.

Internet Access

In the modern times, there is no need to worry about communication. Maybe one of the greatest benefits of coming through the notion of creating passive income is the ubiquity of internet access. These days, you will be able to connect with your business everywhere you are. You may also do it with smartphones, tablets, laptops, and beyond. You will no longer be chained to a desktop, or anything like that. If you desire to move forward into another area, or if you are planning to work from a coffee shop, you will now be able to do so. The point here is that you are in an arena in which the ubiquitous nature of internet allows you to work from anywhere. This alone has been shining light on all the benefits that you can receive from passive income streams.

Freedom of creativity

When you work on a regular job, regardless of how much you love it, it is stifling in a creative way. The average worker in a cubicle will not be free to do anything they want. You should have a method to the work that you should do, and you need to do it with a particular focus on precision. The same goes all over different industries. The more you look in this, the more you will come to realization that your creativity has not been on display. Even artists who work on graphic designing project need to work with creativity relevant to the needs and wants of their clients. You cannot have the freedom outside the notion of passive income, and working from home. If you decide on working from home and want to follow your passions, it is important to be as creative as you want, and spend more time to hone your skills in this arena.

Make money while sleeping

It is the dream, although people think that it is far out of reach – sleeping while getting paid. You will get paid even when you are not doing anything. As a matter of fact, even when you are sitting poolside somewhere out of town, you can get paid while doing nothing but enjoying your life. It is the ultimate benefit of passive income, and there are people who live it every day. There are also people who become bored with this and just wait for a new thing that they can work on.

Freedom to do anything you want

You are entitled to any schedule on those that make money online. As a matter of fact, they make their own schedule. They create their own business entities and they do anything they want. If you want to work for just 2 hours per day, you will be able to create a business model that will elevate you to that. When you have more time to spend with friends and family, and pursue hobbies that you would want to pursue, it is an important thing that many people are not able to do because they have been stuck in traditional jobs. Break that mold and get paid just as much more than your traditional jobs, without investing a full-time schedule toward the working process.

These are just few of all the benefits that you can receive through passive income. Learn what the phases of passive income are to get started living to your freedom while earning money without a need to work for it.

Chapter 3 – How Can a Passive Income be Generated?

Most people can agree that the keystone to success is demanding work and diligence. They're anxious to getting behind the race. These kinds of people have already proven to achieve stability in their life. On the other hand, the lazy ones don't have problem at all become they don't simply have anything to at all as well. Both people have personally chosen to be so. It sounds completely fair, isn't it?

However, nowadays, this equilibrium is a thing of the past. If we have this kind of mindset, then we'll be surprised at the amazing successes of those people have are exerting less effort and at great frustration of those people who have made their best. It doesn't necessarily mean that life is unfair. As a matter of fact, we can now make money not just from what we are doing; which is also known as the active income, but also from what we don't do; which is called the passive income.

Active income is what we can generate from our diligence and demanding work. When we are working to earn money, it's called active income. On the other hand, when it's our own money that is working for is, it's called passive income. The passive income is what we can generate out of our investments. Generating passive income without the active intervention isn't a kind of magic that anyone could possibly have.

If you're wondering how to generate passive income, it happens when our investment earns due to our timely decision. In this kind of income, you are paid for the decision you make as well as for the risk that you have taken. When becoming afraid of investments, you won't be able to make any wise decision. Consequently, nothing will happen to your money. To generate passive, we need to make the best and right decisions on when and what to invest and not decision about making investments. Also, you need to calculate and take risk – if the risk is higher, you will have higher returns. The lower the risk would mean the longer it would take to receive a potential return. It will all depend on who you are and what kind of investment suits your personality.

Proactive kinds of people are naturally career oriented that why they can successfully generate an active income. However, on the other hand, people who are patient enough are wise risk takers and wise decision makers.

Now, which kind of earner you need to be? The active earners have complete control of how much they could possibly earn, but there's a limit in the amount due to their limited time and energy. Once they stop working, so does their income. On the other hand, however, the passive earners are much more efficient because they enjoy the limitless potential of earning high income with less energy. In addition to that, the passive earners can be passive and active earner at the same time. Apparently, the passive earners in terms of efficiency are more advantageous.

It's not hard to know how to start generating passive income. There is many available information around that can help you learn how to get started with this. Generally, we have heard of investing and among the most popular are bonds, stock market, insurance, mutual funds, treasury notes, and pension plans. Before you invest, it's important to learn more about your choice of investment first. You don't need to be the jack of all trades. What's important is that you understand both the potential and risk of the market you want to enter and always start small only for a try. As the time goes by, you will gain the necessary experience and will eventually master the market that you have chosen. In the introduction of the technology, it has become much easier to acquire more information about various field of endeavor. The internet provides numerous tools necessary for you to become well-equipped.

The most important part of generating passive income is your attitude toward the investment. Some would think that investment is made to sustain their daily needs and this is a very wrong notion. If so, it's not anymore an investment, but rather a livelihood. Your immediate needs can just be sustained by the active income. To depend on the investment for you daily need is very irresponsible. You need to work to live and invest at the same time to secure your tomorrow. The real investors are very future-oriented. Hey don't really make money in an instant but their money is the one that makes them. That's the real reason why we are calling this a passive income. Everyone's need today is very different from you needs tomorrow or in the future. Your immediate need should be answered by immediate action and the immediate results can make you grow. However, passive income isn't something that should make you grow. This is something that you should grow. Therefore, whatever you earn now is what you need now. What you do now is the reflection of active income. The right attitude towards passive income is treating it as a separate living entity. What you need now is active income and passive income will be the investment you need now. It's like a pet that you need to raise.

What about having a business? It is active income or passive income? Truth be told, it's the combination of both. The businessman controls the flow of his cash actively to sustain his daily needs and at the same time save some bigger portion for the benefit of his business as a completely separate entity. However, businesses are very complex these days depending on the size. Mostly, the large corporations are owned by several people who are called the stockholders. They are hiring managers and CEOs to control their operations actively. Sometimes, they also intervene in macro level. However, their effort and control are limited compared to the income they receive yearly if the company is continuously growing.

For these kinds of people, these big companies are their main source of passive income. For the small businessmen, they need to exert their entire effort for the growth of their business. They will face trouble in growing their business because they will also depend on active income that they are generating from their operation of their business. Would this conclude that to generate passive income one should have huge capital to invest? Not really. You can do good by simply investing share of stock or even in smaller amounts of money. Also, this is true with the mutual fund that the pool of the individual investment in smaller amounts to make a single huge investment. In other world, you will generate passive income just like the big investors.

Bottom line is you need to learn the ways how to successfully generate the passive income while you are maintaining your active income so you won't compromise the balance between the benefits of both active and passive income. Generating passive income means keeping your active income.

Chapter 4 - Phases Passive Income

There are various definitions of passive income given by many different experts. Generally, building a passive income means that once you've spend your time in creating and developing a stream of income, you need to never go back and worry about it ever again. Theoretically, the passive income that you've worked very hard for will be able to earn you some money over time with little up to no work at all on your part. Rather than spending lots of your time in maintaining this kind of income stream, you can just devote more of your precious time in creating new or additional passive stream of income or probably just spend it in enjoying and relaxing the beauty of life.

If you want to build successful streams of passive income, it would take 3 phases to establish a successful source of income. Here are the level phases involved in passive income:

1. Research – One of the most important steps in building passive income is to conduct a proper research before starting. This is especially true if you need to spend money to create a source of income as an investment. For instance, a newbie may think that they can buy cheap hosting service and domain name for a few dollars as well as in short span of time will be able to create a source of income from a blog or website. A proper research would mean that making an income from a blog or website that's less than one year old is very hard but still, not impossible. Even if it would cost you $0, you need to conduct a research before your completely devote your time to a certain project that might not really work.
2. Build – Once you've conducted a research and you are already comfortable with building a particular stream of income, it is the right time to start building it. The building phase could possibly take you anywhere from a few hours, days up to several years, which would depend on the kind of passive income opportunity you have. Writing and posting an affiliate articles would take you about 15 minutes, while starting a building that would eventually turn you to a manager to run it could take you years before achieving success. The key here is to completely accomplish phase 1, be confident in your own choices and decisions, and proceed to the next phase; maintain.
3. Maintain – This phase is where a lot experts disagree about the meaning of passive income. Regardless of what streams of passive income you've created, there's still some kind of effort in maintaining it to keep the opportunity of earning money passively for you. Even if you're investing in certificate of deposit, it would require you to carefully review the new rates as well as rollover the expired CD into new. While you have minimal time, you must still nurture and maintain a demanding work.

Creating streams of passive incomes can sometimes be very challenging. You need to be aware that not every stream of passive income you create will ensure you success. The key is to completely recognize the things that work and fails as you move forward and make them to your advantage. Your right path to success is to follow these 3 phases of passive income. Regardless of your long-term goals, it's sure enough that we love to be able to create streams of income that can save us time and allow financial freedom. Nowadays, worrying how you're going to pay your next month's bills and your job being in jeopardy can be eliminated. Building passive income isn't east and a get-rich-quick scheme. However, dedication and hard work will surely allow you to reach your goals.

Chapter 5 – Sources of Passive Income

Passive income is one of the most sought after source of income, and it is most commonly misunderstood. Sources of passive income require an upfront investment and lots of nurturing in the beginning. After some challenging work and time exerted, these income sources start building and can maintain themselves, and thus, bringing consistent revenue to you without much effort on your part. In line with this, adding source of passive income to your portfolio will be able to help you in increasing your earnings and accelerating your financial goals in diverse ways.

Passive Income Requiring Upfront Time Investment

This income source is generated through different means, such as Google Adsense, direct advertising, banners and images, and affiliate income advertising. Technically, it is purely passive because people will visit your site to click on the ads. But as a blogger, you will also need to post articles on a regular basis and maintain your website, which requires a lot of work in the beginning. Here are some other passive income sources that require upfront time investment.

- **Selling stock photos:** Are you ever wondering where your blogs, favorite websites, and at times, even magazines get their images? Commonly, you can purchase them from stock photo sites. If you enjoy taking photos, you can submit your photos to stock photo websites and you will receive a commission whenever someone buys one of them.

- **Creating a course on Udemy:** Udemy is an online platform that will let you take video courses on varying aspects. Rather than being a customer on Udemy, you can be a producer, make your own video course, and enable the users to buy it. It can a fabulous choice if you have wide knowledge in a subject. In addition, it can be a fantastic way of turning your traditional tutoring into a source of passive income.

- **Affiliate marketing:** It is the practice to partner with a company and become their affiliate. Here, you will receive a commission on a product. This income generation method works best for those who have websites and blogs. Even then, it will take you a long time to build up before it can become passive. If you are planning to get started with affiliate marketing, there are several marketing programs that you should learn and understand.

- **Selling digital files on Etsy:** If you are into home decoration, you may consider Etsy. You can buy digital files of some artworks that you want to be printed out. The seller created many wall arts, get it digitalized, and listed it on Etsy so that you can download it instantly. You may also find other famous digital files on

Etsy and monthly planners. Especially if you are planning to pursue a career in graphic design, it can be a great passive income idea for you. You just have to exert some time in the beginning.

- **Network marketing:** Multi-level marketing or network marketing has been on the rise these days. You will be able to earn passive income with networking by building a team underneath you, which is usually referred to as your downline. As soon as you have a wide team, you will earn commissions off of their sales without a need for too much to do.

- **Licensing music:** Just as with the stock photos, you may also license and earn royalty from your music when someone decides to use it. Music is usually licensed for commercials, YouTube videos, and others.

- **T-shirt designing:** There are websites that enable users to custom design items like t-shirts. If your design becomes famous and it makes sales, you can earn royalties.

- **App creation:** If have a tablet or smartphone, you most probably have some apps downloaded. However, did you ever had a time when some amazing ideas for an application? If so, you may hire a programmer to make that app for you. Then, you can sell it on Play Store or App Store for some amazing residual income.

Passive Income Requiring Upfront Monetary Investment

Passive income requiring upfront monetary is purely passive income. You don't much effort as soon as you set it up, but it will take lots of initial investment to generate a small percentage of gain.

- **Peer to Peer Lending (P2P):** The P2P lending source of passive income is to loan money to borrowers who are not qualified for traditional loans. As lenders, you can select the borrowers and you can spread the amount of investment to the limit you want, so that you mitigate your risk.

- **Annuities:** These are insurance products that you pay but it provides passive income for life in the form of month-to-month payments. In annuities, the terms vary and these have not always been a great deal so it would be best to talk to a trusted financial advisor if you are interested in buying an annuity.

- **Dividend Stocks:** Dividend stocks have been a tried and true way of earning passive income. There are lots of research necessary to find good stocks, and it is significant to invest a great amount of money if you want to receive large dividend checks. Nevertheless, if you are going to invest money into dividend stocks consistently, you may amass a great residual income as time passes by.

- **Rental properties:** One fabulous way of bringing in a monthly income passively is through a cash flowing rental property. To make this a true source of passive income, you may consider outsourcing the running of the properties to a management company. The greater thing about using a platform as compared to when you are planning to do it yourself, your income will become even more passive.

- **Money Market Funds or CD Ladders:** Establishing a CD Ladder needs buying of CDs or Certificates of Deposits from the banks in specific increments s that you can start earning higher returns on your money. The CDs are usually offered by banks and since they're a low-risk investment, they also give low return. This is a great option for risk averse.

Semi-Passive Small Business

Semi-passive small business is the combination of both passive and active income. The semi-passive income will be the one to continue making money when you're not working, but still requires a certain degree of management or maintenance.

- **Owning a Small Business**: Example of a semi-passive small business is owning a small company. Your business will continue making money even without your presence, but would still require you to check and make some management decisions along the way. The more you put effort into it, the greater your potentials of earning money.

- **Be a Landlord**: You can make semi-passive income every month by becoming a landlord, receiving rent payments, but checking in frequently in order to ensure that everything is as it needs to be, and taking care of potential problems with the tenants or the property. Partially, it's also a long-term investment because you are earning money every month from it and expecting it to appreciate it value over time.

- **Car Wash Business**: starting a car wash business as a source of semi-passive income is a fantastic way to earn money. While the regular maintenance is needed at car wash business it is something that you can perform or hire out just once a week.

- **Vending Machine**: This is another example of minimal maintenance semi-passive small business idea. You just need to replenish and cash out the machine once every two week, and that's it! You have a reliable semi-passive income source.

- **Storage Rentals:** try owning a set of storage rental and you will be able to receive checks every month for letting the customers rent the space out. The only time you must do work for storage rental is when there an opening for one of your storage units.

Easy Passive Income Ideas

If you don't like those that are mentioned above, here are some easy passive income ideas for you to consider. These would require you no money as well as no upfront work. While your earnings will be menial, this is still one of the best income ideas to consider.

- **Cashback Rewards:** If you are paying your bills through credit card, you need to ensure that it is offering cash back rewards. Let your rewards to accrue and put easy money you earned to another passive income project. Note: Make sure that you card you use doesn't have an annual fee or you will only be canceling our the rewards you receive.

- **Cashback Sites:** Just like the cashback rewards on card, you need to choose using a cashback website when you shop online. If you don't you are giving up the free money that needs little to no work at all.

Online Passive Income Sources

There are a lot of opportunities available out there to a make the residual income in the network marketing. However, this isn't one of those traditional passive income sources. Online Passive Income ideas are legit ways for you to make money while you are sleeping in something that suits your passion, skill-set or experience.

- **eBook Selling:** If you do this right, this is quite a lucrative stream of passive income. It would take some effort and time to write and research a good book, but once done well, you can sell it repeatedly for several years to come.

- **Domain Name and Website Selling:** one of the best parts about the online passive income is that a domain name and website is like real estate – Its value can go up over time. As a matter of fact, sometimes only the domain name without the already develop business can be worth much more to some people. It is like nearly anything that is mentioned here, the necessary understanding is needed. If you are willing to invest some time to it, then you can possibly earn nice passive income online. You can sell domain names with price tags of hundreds and thousands of dollars. This is a nice passive income, considering that you can buy a domain name for only $10 and sell it for thousands.

- **Membership Sites:** This is a website that has made a protected member-only access. In other words, the access to all the content on a site is restricted to the registered members only. Developing a membership website is a very powerful way of generating online passive income and scale a service based business. By having the members pay you monthly or other periodic fees to get the access to the password-protected access where the exclusive content is available, you can possibly transform the website into a recurring passive income business and bring regular stream of income from similar customer base.

- **Software:** This is one of the most lucrative ways to earn passive income but most of online businessmen shy away from this due to the technical aspect that's involved in it. Truth be told, you don't need skills in programming to build software. The entire process can be fairly outsourced easily. You only need to know how to choose a good developer and have the winning ideas to the customers that are willing to pay for your service.

- **Release an App to App Store:** While building apps for Android or Apple mobile devices can be a great way to generate a passive income online, it is not easy as it really seems. Aside from the fact that it hard to get your application noticed among millions of apps released every year, most of the people are expecting apps to be either very inexpensive or even free. As a matter of fact, it is found out in a recent study that only 11% of the apps are paid for. The number of the paid apps will continuously decline over time as more and more players will join the market. The key here is to be just like many of business model already mentioned here; be creative and strategic from the very start. There are some ways to monetize your application and keep it free for the users. Example, you can include premium services, advertising, and accept sponsors.

If you will take complete advantage of the opportunities available to you, you need to put your energy, time, effort as well as load of your commitment. The possibilities are starting a passive income are endless; and it has never been very affordable to start a business in human history. So, stop hesitating and start your "one day" today. Choose a passive income stream that you really feel right for you.

Chapter 6 – How to Spot A Passive Income Opportunity

If you're looking for an opportunity to start a passive income you're on the proper track towards building a financial freedom. Oftentimes, passive income is referred to as a smart money and it's the most preferred method where the rich earn their money. Passive income is a kind of income that can be generated continuously even long after your initial work or effort. Literally, you quite get paid repeatedly for the work that you've done once.

Nowadays, there are lots of passive income opportunities available than ever before, both offline and online. Above all, the internet has opened a wide new world with lots of avenues to be explored in virtually in any niche market that you can possibly think of. Spotting a great passive income opportunity can be a little challenging due to the sheer amount of available choices that can be overwhelming.

Basically, there are two great ways to earn passive income online, though it is no exclusively an internet thing. First, you need to build your own idea or product and sell it to someone who will be able to handle the selling and marketing for you. From this, you would earn royalties, which is a reliable source of passive income. Earning royalties is one of the most common passive income in music industry and this can be very lucrative.

You can also earn passive income through other people's idea or products through associate and affiliate programs. You can establish a website, where you will do the work once and start earning recurring income through the affiliate commission. This is just one of various ways you can possibly start passive income online. Probably, the biggest challenge here isn't in finding the opportunity for passive income, but in deciding which one to take. Here are some guidelines to help you spot a great passive income opportunity.

- Be very careful of the over-inflated promises and testimonials. Most of these are only made up. Try to cross-check these testimonials and see if they can really deliver what they promise. If you reach the person providing the testimonial, then is the best way to handle this. There's nothing like genuine advice and answer from someone who's making success from what you're about to go on board.

- Do you responsibly on the company that maneuvers the program. In terms of affiliate programs, you need to stay with big guns such as Linkshare, Commission Junction, and Clickbank, and many other reliable affiliate program, as far as possible. They're less likely to disappear after several years and there's nothing worse than working hard setting up your passive income only to see it disappear after a few years.

- There are a lot of passive income opportunities in hot and fad products, but rarely last a long time. You might really do well for a few months, but would hardly justify the initial effort as well as the prospect of earning the lifetime commission that you could possibly earn. Try and always think 2 years ahead for you to foresee if the product would still be in demand and whether it has god a potential for future growth.

- Be sure to trust and believe in your product. If you don't, then you would never can promote it with the required confidence for you to be successful. Building a passive income needs a great initial effort and it can be difficult to get it start and running. Be sure that it is something that you really love, something that you really believe in and something that is worth spending your time. This is crucial in establishing the necessary motivation for your success.

Keep in mind that a passive income opportunity is just an opportunity until and unless you started to grab it and make action. It is never really about opportunity that really counts, but about what you give and do for that opportunity. Understand that you've everything to gain and nothing to lose. Remember: we tend to regret thing that we don't do. But one thing is for sure: successful passive income can really make you sleep very well at night, without stress and worries.

Chapter 7 – Building Passive Income As an Established Marketer

As an established marketer, you are very likely to have the things that you can plug right away in to achieve passive cash over time. It is only a matter of place the pieces of puzzle together in a way that really works.

To build a passive income as an established marketer, take stock of what you already have. What kind of products you have? What domain names or websites do you have? What kind of internet marketing experience and skills you have already built up? Sometimes people become very complacent of what they have that they already ignore their potential.

Sometimes, you need to look through your list of products and find the best ways on how to give a new life to the old products. Try putting it on its own new domain, reuse content in new places, generate an affiliate interest, and so on. Go through what you already have and think of several ways on how you can possibly turn it into a stream of passive income – or strengthen what it is earning you right now, passively.

One of the most common mistakes a lot of internet marketer make is placing their product up for sale at Forums. That will only get you far. People won't be seeing your product anymore, unless it happens to rank in search engine for one key term, which really work. Place your products on their own domain. Give them a new life, promotion, and chance to passively make earnings for you.

In some cases, you can also take the products you have already create and use them passively as list builders. Place your old yet valuable products up as freebies in exchange of people's e-mail address. This will eventually turn into a stream of passive income for you.

It goes without saying that building a huge email list plays a big part in your success. It is much easier to get the affiliate out there making earnings for you if the people really know you and the quality of work your do. If you are not getting more affiliates, it is the right time to work on the ways you do. You need to do this for better passive income.

Along with selling of products is building bigger email list. If you are not building an email list as you sell your products, you are really missing out a huge opportunity.

Most people can agree that the keystone to success is hard work and diligence. They're anxious to getting behind the race. These kinds of people have already proven to achieve stability in their life. On the other hand, the lazy ones don't have problem at all become they don't simply have anything to at all as well. Both people have personally chosen to be so. It sounds completely fair, isn't it?

However, nowadays, this equilibrium is a thing of the past. If we have this kind of mindset, then we'll be surprised at the amazing successes of those people have are exerting less effort and at great frustration of those people who have made their best. It doesn't necessarily mean that life is unfair. As a matter of fact, we can now make money not just from what we are doing; which is also known as the active income, but also from what we don't do; which is called the passive income.

Conclusion

If you wish to be rich, then you must start generating passive income. Passive income is an income that you don't need to work for when done successfully. You need to build a passive income that is far much greater than your everyday expenses.

A lot of people define the word "rich" differently. Some want to have a million dollar in their bank, some want to have a mansion, and some want to travel around the world. But, whatever your definition of rich is, one thing is for sure; to be rich you must generate some passive income. Passive income will be the one to fund your lifestyle and help you to afford the best things that you want in life, help you pay for the food, mansion and entertainment that you desire. Ultimately, it will also fund you everyday lifestyle so you don't need to work for money, but instead have the money work for you.

The End

Also, Check Out This Other Book Published by Success Publishing

Startup Blueprint

Free Preview Bonus

Automatic Income Machines: e-Business Blueprint

With an economic whiplash that hits most the countries today; more people are joining ranks in achieving economic progress through the internet. The internet world had become an American Dream while others look at it as the other side of the world with the greener pasture.

Many had indeed taken their chance in starting an online business, yet not all are ready to face all the challenges and the complexities of surviving in the internet business arena.

However, for those who were lucky enough to survive, they lived to testify to the kind of life online business offers.

This "e-Business Blueprint" aims to provide beginners with a guide on setting up an online business and guiding you through the simple steps to achieve success.

With proper knowledge and determination, success on any online business can be achievable and in fact, rewarding. It's just a matter of planning and driving you towards a goal that can really make your dream comes true.

CHAPTER 1: Reasons for Getting Into an Online Business

People got different reasons for going into online business. But most often, online business is for people who got tired of working 8-5 or 9-6 every day. Rushing each morning for a gulp of coffee before fighting his way through traffic and hoping he could be earlier than usual!

As you realized that you are getting tired of working for someone else and you want to become your own boss, you start thinking of the possibility to make it big in the internet business. Hoping, you are right, and then the best way to set up a business with a greater chance to make it to success is to start now!

Here are just a few of the many reasons why you must start with your internet business.

Goodbye to Traffic and Early Morning Rush

With an internet business, you don't need to rush up too early that you need to skip eating breakfast just so you can arrive in time for work. But when you are living in an overcrowded metropolis where you had to go through jam-packed traffic, stress and anxiety can be a daily part of your routine!

Online business can help you save a lot of money by not traveling every day. Count the savings you can have when you don't need to go out for work. You can likewise save your time and convert the time spent for daily trips into more productive inputs.

No Need Putting Up with a Toxic Boss

Most often people got fed up and want to get out of their work because they have a toxic person for a boss. Most often, bosses thought that their employees are there to please them all the time. This often happens when you are working in a sole proprietorship type of business or a one-man organization. Most often than not, you feed to your boss whims and schemes rather than get productive in your tasks. In the end, you feel thoroughly burnt out and find a quick way to change job.

Working at your own Pace and Time

When you are running an online business, you can be your own boss. You can work at a chosen time and place. You can even have more time to yourself and to your family. However, this can have its own drawback. So, before you get out of your work, be sure your finances or the lack of will not cripple you. Proper timing is needed so your family will not suffer from your decision.

When you are free to decide for yourself whether you are going to work or not, be sure you manage your time effectively and efficiently. When you're alone to manage your time and no one is around to put pressure on you, you don't give yourself a reason to procrastinate. You need to learn to balance everything even without someone to answer to. Remember that every minute wasted is an opportunity lost in online business.

Unlimited Income Potential

Working on a regular career means putting up a cap on how much you can earn. But with online business, your ability to earn depends on how much time you want to put into your business. You can earn as much or as little as you want. The market for online business is too vast. You just learn to tap its unlimited resources and you go as far as you can.

You can target people around the world as the global market is getting bigger and bigger and more people are learning how to access the internet every day. You can work as much or as little as you choose. The marketplace for internet businesses is worldwide.

Per the later report of the Statistics portal, the number of internet users had risen up to 3.17 billion this year from 2.94 of the previous year. Doesn't that market large enough to dip your toes into?

Minimal Expenses for an Office

Since you are working from the comfort of your home, you don't need to rent an office space. You will again be saving a lot on your administrative expenses compared if you are running a conventional type of business.

In setting up your business, all you need to have is your laptop or PC and low-cost hardware and software which you can even get for free online if you're just diligent enough to browse through your internet.

Bigger Chance to Achieve more for Less Work

An online business allows you to work fewer hours and achieve more. There are some business models that can be fully automated. You just must set them up and (lo!), they can run on their own and earns you a passive income. This automation process now is widely used in the internet market. If you can't run your business on 100% automation, you can at least have it automated at 50% or more, so you can have more time for additional business to carry on.

What makes an online business unique than conventional ones is you can operate multiple businesses single-handedly. To simplify, you are operating a business that is almost next to impossible – Less capital, less time, and less effort for unlimited income streams potentials.

Common Problems you will Encounter at the Start of your Online Business

Starting your online business can be both rewarding and stimulating. However, you are sure to encounter a few problems that new entrepreneurs usually encounter. To steer clear of these issues, you must be aware of them and avoid them as they come along.

Tempting Opportunities and Resources

As you start hanging on the internet, you will be meeting a lot of opportunities along with remarkable resources to promising you great support in your online business. These products, usually software or a business opportunity, may be as great as their vendor advertise them. Nonetheless, if you jump from one opportunity to another, you will be losing your focus on your core business. It is, therefore, important that you start an online business with only what you absolutely need and have it run smoothly before getting into another. The same works with your software or any other tool.

Neglecting New Opportunities

Basically, this is the exact opposite of grabbing every opportunity that comes along. If you refuse to examine or look at any new opportunity sent your way because you have your focus set up trying to achieve a goal with a method that simply don't work, avoid overlooking the warning signs that tell you that you need to move on or move in another direction.

Doing Everything by Yourself

When you think it's better to keep all the profit, you keep trying to do everything so you can keep the money to yourself. Saving is always good for your business, but as your business develops, it will become impossible for you to embrace all the tasks. This is the time when you need to develop some way to ease up your workload. An example of these if subscribing for an auto responder that will take care of your mailing activities. Instead of manually sending letters, answering queries, the auto-responder allows you to maintain and develop relationships with your customer base and up-sell or cross-sell your products and services.

Having Too Many Choices

Affiliate marketing is a good start for an online business for you can earn as soon as someone buys from your inks. This is the reason why it is so popular with many people. Affiliate marketing method has many positive aspects but there are too many choices that it is confusing to know which to promote. Before you jump into marketing a new software by way of an affiliate program, check how much commission you can earn from it, how you can get paid, and know if there is some support you can get from the owner. It is also important to know if the product sells before promoting it.

The Internet is Bigger than What You Think

Having an online business doesn't mean that people will naturally visit your website and buy things that you offer. The internet is such an enormous marketplace that you need to know how to get prospective customers to visit your visit so you can have the chance to convert these visits into sales. Meaning, you need to learn how to generate website traffic by utilizing both free and paid traffic generators.

No Support from Family and Friend

Sometimes, we presume that our family and friends will be our loyal customer. Sad to say, in most cases, it doesn't usually happen especially during the start of your business. There are even cases when they will discourage you from doing online business. Though these people mean well, don't get easily swayed and let your goals and efforts get destructed. If you have set your goal and created a business plan to back it up, you have every opportunity to get successful.

Regardless of whom you are, your age, gender, technical skills, educational background, you can always start your own internet business. You can always harness whatever skill you have through various learning platforms and resources provided on the internet for a certain fee or for free.

Download Startup Blueprint NOW!